At
the
Western
Gates

Also by Nathaniel Tarn

Poetry

Old Savage/Young City (1964) / *Where Babylon Ends* (1969)
The Beautiful Contradictions (1969; 2nd edition 2013)
October (1969) / *The Silence* (1969)
A Nowhere for Vallejo (1971) / *Section: The Artemision* (1973)
The Persephones (1974; revised editions, 2008, 2016)
Lyrics for the Bride of God (1975)
The House of Leaves (1976; 2nd edition 2018*) / *The Microcosm* (1977)
Atitlán / Alashka [Alashka with Janet Rodney] (1979)
Weekends in Mexico (1982) / *The Desert Mothers* (1984; 2nd edition 2018*)
At the Western Gates (1985; 2nd edition 2018*)
Palenque: Selected Poems 1972-1984 (1986)* / *Seeing America First* (1989)
Home One (1990) / *The Army Has Announced That Body Bags…* (1992)
Caja del Río (1993) / *Flying the Body* (1993) / *The Architextures* (2000)
Three Letters from the City: The St. Petersburg Poems (2001)
Selected Poems: 1950-2000 (2002) / *Recollections of Being* (2004)
Avia (2008)* / *Ins & Outs of the Forest Rivers* (2008)
Gondwana and Other Poems (2017)
Alashka [with Janet Rodney] (first separate publication, 2018)*

Translations

Pablo Neruda: *The Heights of Macchu Picchu* (1966)
Pablo Neruda: *Selected Poems* (1968) / Victor Segalen: *Stelae* (1969)
Con Cuba (1969) / *The Rabinal Achi, Act 4* (1973)
The Penguin Neruda (1975)

Prose

*Views from the Weaving Mountain:
Selected Essays in Poetics & Anthropology*, 1991
Scandals in the House of Birds: Shamans & Priests on Lake Atitlán, 1998
*The Embattled Lyric:
Essays & Conversations in Poetics & Anthropology*, 2007

* *from Shearsman Books*

Nathaniel Tarn

At the Western Gates

Shearsman Library

Second, expanded edition. First U.K. publication.
Published in the United Kingdom in 2018 by
The Shearsman Library
an imprint of Shearsman Books
50 Westons Hill Drive
Emersons Green
BRISTOL
BS16 7DF

Shearsman Books Ltd Registered Office
30–31 St. James Place, Mangotsfield, Bristol BS16 9JB
(this address not for correspondence)

www.shearsman.com

ISBN 978-1-84861-587-8

Copyright © Nathaniel Tarn, 1976, 1985, 2018.

The right of Nathaniel Tarn to be identified as the author of this work
has been asserted by him in accordance with the
Copyrights, Designs and Patents Act of 1988.
All rights reserved.

Front cover glyph by Nathaniel Tarn and John Brandi.
Interior glyphs by Nathaniel Tarn.

ACKNOWLEDGEMENTS
First published in 1985 by Tooth of Time Books,
Sante Fe, NM, containing the first five sequences.
'Birdscapes with Seaside' first published as a solo issue
of *Sparrow* magazine by Black Sparrow Press, 1976.

The Landsongs first appeared as a Blue Guitar chapbook –
and also as part of an issue of *Shearsman* magazine – one of the earliest
publications by Shearsman Books – in 1981.

Contents

Journal of the Laguna de San Ignacio   9

Further Annotations
    from Baja California: The Landsongs   25

Jonah's Saddle   35

Palenque   51

North Rim   61

Birdscapes with Seaside   94

Publisher's Note   104

At the Western Gates

for Janet Rodney

Journal of the
Laguna de San Ignacio

Immense architecture
building in air
towers and palaces
from which their eyes look out,
star denizens
living in the heights
as they live below
building in air
and undersea
their passage through our life –
        a gentle glide
like a dream
because no thing men know
so huge and gentle at once
can be other than dream
        in such a world.
Whales breathing
all around us in the night
just beyond the lights,
ghost gulls
following the ship
which seems to breathe
yet never moves
against the great Pacific's
unfathomable shoulders

The mountains rise out of the desert
way out over Baja
the whales rise out of the sea
the mountains rise out of the sea
the whales rise out of the desert
the whales are taller than the mountains

There was a man one time
got buried in a whale they say,
found bed and board down there
also some breakfast,
found desk and library
and was granted extra knowledge
    (the whale a shaman they say).
        Cast from the human city,
he went down to the sea in whales
clothed with all his grave clothes
collected over the years
complete with turquoise necklace
– and jadeite necklace
and one bead of jade –
his body full of sweet winds,
      he lay inside the whale
and wrote, in his death, terrible hymns
which no amount of pain
had ever torn from him,
wrenched from his mouth
out through his teeth
        in his mind's hearing

Touching the skin of water
as it glides against water
slow slip of time
the black flesh gleaming like a hull
        (they call it Grey)
mottled with barnacles,
the imaginary touch
which men could have touched for centuries
           (instead of the carnage)
as it took them so long
to come to the beaches
to come to the sea
to come to the mountains

Birds of America
we rendezvous with all of you
in Baja of the sweet blue skies
streaked with the grey and sand.
       From south you call,
       from north,
       up and down your flyways,
and visit here, on the desert floor,
where my love is collecting shells,
    shells of one kind
       Mound of Venus shells,
and laying them out in a pattern
facing into the wind
as if she were making a book
for birds to read.
       All morning she is at it
peacefully, like a worker,
while I walk my fears
from one beach to another
stilling them with the sight of birds.
  At the end,
she places three pelican plumes
at the head of her pattern
facing the Santa Clara mountains.
The very next tide
will take this prayer
back to the sea

Vagaries of the sea life.
My bunk is so short
I need to lose head or feet
and its sky is so low
I have to be fitted into it
like a dime into a slot machine.
If you come into the cabin
you break my back,
if I come in, I break yours.
We have bruised elbows.
Nowhere to sit and read,
the lights don't work.
Water floods in the basin.
And how the hell we get to fuck in here
is any circus animal's guess

Dazzle of light
pale mountains, pale dunes
pale clouds on pale blue skies
immense skullcap of light over the whole,
      the sea fetching sighs
 under the skiff,
his heart
folded among the sea's pages –
   from the depths coming up
 in musical surf
arched bow of the whale
 the vertebrae
shining through skin
circling the skiff
passing, they say,
the flukes over his head
so fast he did not see them
(though they were larger than his houseroof)
but felt the hair on his head
lie down which the wind had raised.
   And the heart came up also
which, in its fear,
the sea had previously bound into its secrets

Forest of whales,
Lebanon cedars
with their roots in the sea
sparring,
looking down at leisure
on the human world.
Forest of heads
above the prophet
in his rubber coffin,
laid out with all his jewels
tight round his neck,
his escaping soul's
breath still alive
is the finest mist
among the clouds of spray
from the cruising whales,
you will recognize it

Our lives collapse,
houses of water,
as the whale glides
up out of water
smooth and exact
with no effect beyond
its perfect fit
into eight million years
each passage like the last.
Our childish history
expires into a sky
so vast it has no edges

Lagoons in space
enclosed like wombs,
satellites of earth,
wide mirrors receiving
the planet's music,
star songs
in well-tuned skies.
Far out in space,
warmed by the sun,
fry, bubble, sizzle,
in silver-wrap
the celestial whales:
down drip of blubber
(deluge of calm)
turning in our sphere
every sign of the zodiac
to their own favor

Whales wild this morning
and skittish,
waves lapping against skiffs,
the skiffs rocking,
and animals preparing
for the voyage north,
taking longer to rise
between their breaths

& how come no fear
in this roiling –
dragons among the waves,
behemoth / leviathan,
close as domestic pets?
  If they barked, I think,
as loud as their size suggested,
childhood would tower
out of all proportion,
the world's walls
would cave in,
the floor break earthquake:
I would probably not
enter this lagoon
in a battleship!

"Though they take me down
into the freezing wave,
though they drop me naked
into the invisible,
and I cry there
for any voice to answer –
one voice out of the void –
and no voice sounds,
while leviathan
rises from below
his mouth agape
to take me in his body,
though they kill me and cut me to pieces
to feed me to that whale:
still I sing,
still do not keep quiet,
they have a singer
on their hands
and a voice
talking, singing, praying,
they cannot quench
if only the sun returns
to bless the earth like this
once in the centuries
between each of my breaths"

"Perhaps it is not the sea
we have witnessed
raising these whales
to the power of air
and downing them again to depths
unheard of in the history of water –
        perhaps it is the sky,
even paradise,
    and these are the heavenly animals
with wings of wind and music
who have laid their image
on all earthly souls
(since nothing is forgotten.)"
Father, the gate is open
     he declared on landing.
Wrote on that desk
and in that book they say
that was the oldest in the library
     within the belly of the whale:
        "these are the animals
the ancient men,
blind leading blind,
in the old days, on the old ships
with perfumed masts,
hearing the music of the sirens
            thought to be angels…"

Further Annotations from Baja California : The Landsongs

Summit of San Benitos,
light,
three peaks ahead
above surf-wash,
the sea's grey fingers,
the sea's blue fingers
intertwined,
light / light
halo of fire
cholla / firkin / agave
simplicity
of the earth smiling
on this one day of the year:
I can stomach life
inside this crossing
which is my body –
light, air, fire,
under my seat the earth
like a throne,
the desert turned to gold
by alchemical rains
and I the king of it

Exquisite butterflies
small painted ladies
so quick, sassy
it is as if the eye had seen them

Ice flower:
slim daisies
trimmer than fashion models,
candy leaves
you could grate your teeth on,
alien ice flower
come to Baja
to colonize the islands
and marry rocks.
There they are
in the boontime rains
scintillating
among sun flowers
and painted ladies,
drunk on light and air
like the crazy virgins

"You have not heard it,
you have not understood
this blessing.
      You are not there to hear.
         If this
day ever reaches you, that is
if anything whatsoever reaches you
      out of this sun
where the whales call
      from the wide lagoons"

Losing those glasses finally
on San Martin –
name of the Lord of animals
in my birthplace –
which I had lost so often
& found again in other places
through at least three summers.
                But in any case
see now with whale eyes,
ospreys' and voles'.
Human senses fail,
I sniff the human odor
and turn from it
towards the swelling world
out of our line of sight.
A final heirloom:
the savannah sparrow
I remember described
as a nondescript bird
mists over like a jewel
and drops into my ear
(brushing an eyebrow with a wing)
his string of faded pearls

"Suddenly
he forgot that I was alive
& spoke of me in my presence
as if I were dead.
Reading my future
and telling me of loss.
            Far off
a noise of breakers
through which a whale
taking the night apart with method
denied all possibility of day,
filtering star-like shrimp
through her baleen as tall as towers.
Fragments of action. Of any action"

"Canyons in which
I have walked on the floor of the sea
feet firm on sand,
hands
fluttering in disbelief
along rock walls,
eyes full of cholla flowers
mammillaria flowers,
the goddess-nipples
        spiky today,
nostrils cool with the odor
sunlight draws from feathery palms,
rich banks of succulents
along the interface of sand and water.
Underfoot,
stone is hard
and unforgiving as a dying prophet.
Oh, death might come now
to the ball of the eye
and take these feet
back to their golden pavements!
Out front
great walls of surf
as wide as her arms
who mothers the sea and all its creatures
among which whales play in the mind
sounding along its convolutions
and breaching into the clear air of genius:
where they cover the mother's bosom,
her naked splendor with their wings"

"Another sorrow.
One more defeat.
Another death.
The sea's outside,
distant waves
breathe in all other sounds.
Suddenly I meet the beauty of my poems
whom I had never seen bridal before.
I live with them as man and wife
outmarried by death only.
There is no other house"

Jonah's Saddle

ONE

Whose are these voices?
The whale-woman's hair is grey:
she has just come into the room
in which all my friends are buried
    up to the neck.
        They do not sing out
    "Thar she blows!"
their voices shut into their mouths
    by smiling teeth.
One man is talking to his friends
because this is an evening for rapping
        but I don't hear him
    talking about his desert
        who am not his friend
    nor am likely to be, and,
(little holy wind blowing through this soul)
  nor am likely to be of his mind.
Now.
This work is husbandly
and concentrates on the woman
through a cold climate
as we pass from one side of the continent
    to the other.
                Ice
    in Chicago thirty years ago
        (the voice's youth
            muffled in blubber)
    covers the Arizona sands.
                We have been
from band to band of the desert
    and the woman inside me
is alone speaking, and I hear
her voice riding on the voice of the rapping man
                and no other voice

    except perhaps
the howl of a newborn wolf
                        on a deserted beach
as he gets ready
    padding over the sand
to drown into a sea of ice and to change lives

TWO

Whose is the divine voice,
who is mistress of whales on the other side
           of the morning wind?
Wasting the knowledge
the rapping man might give
in order not to listen
to any other knowledge than hers.
There was clearly a marriage below that belt.
    To analyze
           what whales mean
                  when he is talking merely of horses,
to translate
           horses into whales –
divine cavalcades with hoofs of water –
           could no more be done
                         in this mixed company
than to play a tape of Neptune's farts.
           What a divine blessing!
Whales glide up the morning wind
and on a thousand pages of transcript
                         modulate her breath
stroking the waves of the lagoon.
                         The ancient gods
reach for their daily business,
clamber out of bed
blowing noses between fingers,
                         assemble whales
to sing in chorus on the cresting tide
where the sea greets San Ignacio:
    Oh aged prophet,
swallowed by our great fish,
                  the fish of Empire,
    turn your glorious voice into light,
kiss the woman's lips below her belt

    with the smell of sliding water,
now lodge your tongue into your birth-place
    and hear your repertoire!
There. Now.
    Is *that* not worth the crossing?

THREE

We didn't include the music.
                      An ideal would be
to take the vocables of life
                      and weave them to the whales
deaf in the deep
    with their naked language
                           perfectly
   misunderstood.
To go in at the ear,
to generate the marvel of that song,
(his back turned to us
as the back of God is,
in the ancient stories,
away from his brother gods
that we be not afrighted,)
                      to bear the question
whether to issue at the rear
in a boom of bubbles, oil
    rising to surface as if all our wells
had blown their tops at once,
                      this would have to be
the subject for a grant proposal.
    But we must not make public
this ceremony of the dive. / Let me sing to you
    the brackets only.
                      (I am going to tape).
   He is singing only the whale songs.
But the whole of creation is in question.
    Or more precisely: all creativity.
       They are a fragment
           of quite a marvelous poem:
                          mind
         picking out stones
                  in step by step

    transit down stream,
   the hardest work we know:
 same work as following the voice
     rides on another's voice.
And while the whales glide up the morning wind
  all ears are closed.
Mastery towers, however, above all voices.
   Hear them or not:
   Amen. Let it be so.

FOUR

Here in another state
    with their voices they are calling him
who is about to hear
    infinite modulations
of star child / moon child
                singing
    high above whales
sleeping on the waters of San Ignacio
              with their backs
appearing every once in a while
    moon-mirrors,
        gleam of wet blubber –
in another state
        soul at liberty, now, at some rest, now
            purchased from death
                many times over.
        She said the mangroves
around San Ignacio
would reverberate in us
their trunks full of herons
all the water birds
    along these beaches
             our royal aviary!
Voice
that had been sand all year
streaming out of these stems,
fluent mangrove fingers
and the bow like a necklace now, friendly,
                pliant.
        But it *is* the bow, the same
shone out in ancient time on the old world
    gives out the voice
    gives out the deafness
    to the human with its choice of ears!

                    Masterful strings
voice in the jade, the turquoise,
            all you'll do is say...

FIVE

     Little world
           of plankton
let me touch you
with underwater lips.
With their voices for me they are calling
        neighs the horse song over and over,
not in the voice of my friend who wrote it
       but in an alien voice,
    before I am scooped
        by the immense maw of the whale,
    high as a tower
       with the drawbridge open
and all the grass goes in,
      all the dawn pollen.
    (White shells the horses' teeth).
The city dies
for lack of people,
no people / no prophet :
he is taken away,
discharged redundant.
          Strike up the variations.
    Keep faithful
    to the sands,
     take in all wings
     fluttering above the beach:
with their voices for me they are calling,
    and birds for me are calling…
          And the whale rises to me
   out of the nightmare
turning all else into faded grass,
    discoloring pollens,
threshing up bird wings into the chaff

SIX

What is NOT song?
What will dare
          NOT become song?
Will grass
        refuse to become song?
Will flowers?
           Will fish
not become song
making a speech in poetry?
(leave us *one* song to ourselves
    they might say
and give us all *your* poetry!)
Will the animals
     not become song?
What will pack-rat do,
red rattlesnake,
fox on the desert's edges:
will they refuse to become song?
    And what will deer do –
will they shy away from song
     and hide among thickets
on the other side of the lagoon?
          And the whale,
as long as the wall of China,
     will the whale herself
not become song?

SEVEN

How long will it be
before the desert catches fire
and the sea comes home
with all its fellow creatures?
Your voice over the hill
as you shape shells into a pattern,
your grey parka beside you,
pointing towards the arctic
gives me an answer,
shaping our common mind,
and takes me back
    to the cool evening we met
and the whole of solitude lay between us.
    But:
how did it happen
that the waters parted and we met?
    Shy. You said. Timid. Shy.
This discussion has gone on far too long
and the rapman has no more to say.
We are moving into an era of meaningless
    question and polite, political answer.
There is hardly anything left to listen to.
                    You hint at me
it is time to recuperate, in enemy discourse,
    each friendly sound.
How forgiving we must yet grow:
    can we really make it?
Unless, of course: No Enemy.
    Meanwhile, sand turns to gold
      as it cascades
        towards the lagoon
          and breaks against waves.
    Now waves are solid
      and sand flows like water.

Ah, dear god, give us the night out of thy bounty
if thou art bountiful, little-case god, and if not
let it be the desert of our misunderstanding then,
           but at least *our* desert.

(Optional finale:)

In another moment,
    we may yet meet,
in another moment,
    we may yet consummate,
      with just another effort,
         the canopy may be erected
and the room be full of sea, sands, pearls,
    waves breaking over our ears
and whales singing out on mountain tops with birds
            breathing our air again!

In another moment,
     when the sun shines out of the clouds
    yes, sand will catch fire,
we shall make speech,
     we shall meet in the fire

Palenque

*In memory of Denis Pulston,
taken by lightning, Chichén Itzá, June 1978*

"Let the order of ideal time
be asserted and let me
be at the center in the
fire which is still
and does not consume":
an aging man
walking up a steep street,
his mouth on the move
as if he were speaking.
The city he walks is four hundred
and fifty years old – add him
for half a millennium.
It is a place he first came
out of the center to, the first time,
a quarter century ago,
and from here he is going now
to the center again
for the third time.
In the photographs
of the city taken in those days,
there are, even in empty streets,
shadows against walls but no people.
He sees the trees
surrounding Santo Domingo so tall
they are as tall as the trees of
the imagination of his childhood,
as he walks backwards in time
with his neck to the future
like a victim. The house walls
of this city are low
but fall still further inwards
when entered into,
gardens of inner light
his adolescence loved
where his native country
bathed in her body liquids
at the very center of the earth.

Later: they moved that navel
of earth and sky many times,
his own centers shifted,
taking over every quarter of the globe.
He was an empire, you might have said,
to himself – though a silent one,
little publicized: no cult centers,
no tourist venues. In the gardens,
there are enough lilies to bury all poets,
first and foremost the poet fool enough
to decree that one garden be all white
(the one he lived in)
against the natural miscegenation of colors.
In *his* city, there was to be
no racism, the aging man decreed –
he was tired of all
that reminded him of difference,
the record-keeping of difference,
the separating sessions,
the various faces of time. "Let it all
behave together now and not have me
trying to put salt like a child
on a sparrow's tail" seemed to say
the voice of the man coming upstreet
to the domes with snakes in their hair
and inharmonious bells.
Inside the aging man,
there is a young man running
in all directions at once, trying to reach
at breakneck speed, and simultaneously,
what the older man tries to reach slowly
if he wishes to reach it at all.
The younger man has eyes
full of light and his heart
balances the weight of all he'll give
to that light's source when he meets it.
The young man wakes early

to be first in a bus line
for distant mountain villages
on fiesta days when they light up the church
like a living heart. He has spent
all night calculating how many
ravishing textiles he can afford
from a store in the Calle Gabriela
the morning after next.
He also has his eye
on a new edition of the *doings of conquest*
which may cost him a meal or two
if he is going to hit every fiesta
and buy every one of those textiles.
The older man wearies fast
with the comings and goings
of the younger man inside him
so that he finds it difficult
to bite exactly on his own aspirations.
"The order of ideal time *may* be approaching,
it is possible poets do *not* have the exact
knowledge of their own life's courses the way I
think they do, from birth to death"
he whispers to himself, coming up hill,
towards Comitán 7 where he is staying
without much rhyme or reason.
He has a habit
of landing up more often than he used to
in places unrelated to himself.
"Hill goes up, hill goes down: same street"
he thinks to himself as he enters the house.
It could be explained why he lives on Comitán
this weekend, and it could even be made
interesting in that the wife
of another poet, a famous one,
twice married to him / twice divorced, vies there
with sanity, and loses daily.
"I should therefore be doing something

a little more precise than my daily program,
I should be able to
make up my mind whether to move
backwards or forwards from here
if, I mean, backwards or forwards *signifies*
in a dedicated life."
"Why", some one had asked him, on the day before
"why, having done something as good, professionally,
as – citing some article in a Textbook – you should
change names, countries, jobs,
leave family and children,
disappear like a thief in the night"
his could-be colleague had asked, then, jumping:
"but you *are* changing courses again now,
that is visible" the colleague said, and our man:
"As to changing courses (with marked fa-
tigue) "no, merely pushing this course a little,
what is already there, don't you see,
and stressing this a little instead of that,
but, change,
deflecting courses, no, I think not",
whereupon the could-be colleague,
asked about politics of land and oil
knew very little about a major airfield to the south
or the size of a related army base:
they were on the wrong scale of analysis.
The only thing our friend could get his teeth into
was that they were destroying in the south
a place he had always felt to be a candidate
for the exact belly-button place;
it was being destroyed with high-rise,
appropriation of Native lands and jobs,
golf clubs, air strips, floating hotels,
condominiums of senior citizens of his own country
and of the country in which the place stood.
"Perhaps" he thought, as he went into his room,
"it would be good to try to save the place"

which was a lake, and stood up inside his memory
every time he thought of it, as if a wall
of water had stood up inside his head,
draining all else.
If there were nothing other to believe in,
at least this could be done for other peoples'
children, if not his own.
Now, at the invocation
of the lake being saved, the buildings bombed
or otherwise pulled down, against development,
against all likelihood, the volcanoes
going back to their pristine
mirroring of themselves in the lake,
cloud-fingers at dawn unseen by anyone
except the workers in the smoking villages,
another place he had recently come from
rose to his mind, a place he had tried
in his youth to get to, twenty five years before,
and failed because of empty pockets.
It was the year exactly
the belly of the earth was being opened
and a huge stone, down in the underworld,
gave birth to the city's king,
enabled our scholars to name him,
to have some bite on him,
and out of this was dawning,
even among the driest minds,
(like an emergence from that first earth,
or from a conch shell – the history of music –
or from the smoke in the gods' cigars
when they'd been smoking stars all night)
a confluence of such knowledge, breaks in the code
of such a magnitude, that not only this city,
but all the cities round about, the whole empire,
was perhaps about to be understood.
And, so many years later,
with a fatter purse, he had at last been able

to go there. "This people" he had thought
as he approached the place
at long long last:
older and older buses,
the place being far
away from anything,
mule trains for days,
a strip in the jungle,
a small plane lifting him
high into rain-cloud,
flying like that for hours
to the limits of fuel,
before leap-frogging a last ridge,
banking sharply over a river,
two macaws flashing,
red, yellow, blue from monotonous trees
under the wings, the pilot, an artist,
putting him down with a whisper in the forest
and the forest closing over him for days.
All around him the trees had risen
much taller than the walls of Comitán,
even taller than the trees around Santo Domingo,
which look now like the tallest on earth,
and, above the trees, palaces had soared
at the top of immense stairways
weeping down into jungle
stone tears through maidenhair
and other exquisite deep plants.
There, he said later to a very few,
he had witnessed events
unrecorded in any history and not
to be put down on paper by anyone
at any time henceforward.
Flying back, in and out of rain,
from the imperial place, he had believed
he might be able to link past and present together
as no one in any discipline seemed able to do.

It would take a heavy investment of time,
perhaps a dozen dialects, he calculated,
and that would keep him occupied for such
remaining days as he had left
– before the reign of ideal time he clamored for –
but it would also be worth doing
for the sake of others' children,
to the outermost children
and limit of mankind, why not: *such* heroism!
He could save a place,
save a culture,
link one culture relevantly with another,
perhaps with all others: many things undreamed of yet
might be possible from here, and
"Why should I know them now, in advance",
he asked (an old temptation,
moving out of Comitán 7
and about to go into Dr. Navarro 5, the house he had
been asked to sit about a week,
and, from it, you could see the trees
of Santo Domingo, and the garden was drowning in white
lilies everywhere you looked – plus
he had been given a bird, for this chosen time,
Mountain Diglossa – "then, why this bird
rather than any other" he asked himself,
"but it is pleasant,
rather unusual after all, why should I complain:
bluebird colors, sharp beak, long legs,
about 4 inches, works inside fuchsia bushes,
and I have never seen it anywhere before."
He passes first the old Native beggar
he passes every day, promising that on the last
day of his stay, or his half century,
whichever comes first,
he will drop into his astonished hat,
the man being blind, a larger note than usual,
"something being accomplished this way at least"

he thought to himself as he found again
the princess he had failed to find in the imperial city,
though all he had met had told him of her
another hundred unrecordable stories:
"Oh the burden of recorded time," he thought,
"how it wearies, how it consumes me,"
(here nearly breaking into Handel as a joke),
"how it keeps me from that home I have always
known the place of, (but lost the key so often,
or deed, or right of entry) – lost to so much
FOOLISHNESS" he hollered all of a sudden, as
he went through the door, causing a scatter
among the grackles, and the princess laughed, "So
let the order of ideal time" he repeated
"be asserted and let me
be at the center
now without ever leaving it
in the fire which is still and does not consume."

San Cristóbal de las Casas, Mexico.

North Rim

*…to the Body in whose North
I am but Shadow…*

Waiting for you to return
as I wait for this land to return to me
in a small boat under Nellie Juan
           (as well as anywhere)

    the glacier calves:
             a maternal wave
  shatters against the cliffs,
          a sickle movement,
  and rounds on us
            nearly sweeping us back.

In the hot shower
              you swamp my body:
limbs dissolve and drown
              in the gulf of your mouth

The moon cries into the water.
                      Your absence
bleeds into my stay here, but:
            it is not possible
to be awkward in this longing any more
than it is to be uneasy before a flower.
                   Bend over me kindly
wherever you are in this land
and run like a river into the water
                our eyes distressed
together. I want your flow of heart.

Surfing with the birds
over stone and driftwood
bone and sinew of old ships
        wrecked on this coast
into the forest over which the eagle
        gibbers and yelps his calls
strangely unregal,
I drown in the huge salads of Southeast.
Over the fallen woods and down the moss
I run my hand as I would run it
over your spars, over the fragile sails
your hands would make
        if they were travelling here
moving across my limbs
floating the forest to the sea again,
        turning memory down…

On the crowded ship
        all passengers asleep
in their old age,
        eat crab, drink whiskey
with the crew –
then, at midnight,
while youth keeps the show alive,
        drop to the empty cabin,
smell my own armpits undressing,
        bears roaring in my cups –
the sharp scar of your absence
        as I stagger to a narrow bunk:
if there were an odor on the wind,
        clean as an arctic storm outside,
it would be the animal I adore in you
        with his teeth in my muscle
to the stop of bone

Singing for you
in the old voice newly returned,
page after page darkens
with the script of your body,
              we are caressed
by a contingency as sharp
              as a whale's watch
(cavorting round the ship
              so it would seem
and for our seeming pleasure):
but I know the whale at his business
in buried kelp
as I know my voice and recognize
we are the only beings in the world
              to satisfy a longing
not even the stars know about
              as the ship starts out again
on her determined journey,
taking all the paths she knows
and weaving them
into the trackless waste we are
              outside ourselves

Last year's mountains
thrust their jagged peaks
    into the Valdez sky
named after some old Spaniard
    sailed by here years ago
and then forgot his name and Valdez both –
    but I remember all.
               I keep the night awake
for my own use
    and the track of my poem
knows of no destinations
    except the names
I call you by,
baptizing you with all the terms of want:
    my unquenchable desire
rocked on the ocean
by all the flowers opening in dreams
I cannot dream yet, waiting for you

I would write you
into the pages of this sea
if I were captain in some charge
            of my own fate:
but I am like a ship
            without command
and without officers, or destination.
            Turn, woman of
my star searching for home
        and bring this page to
    unravelled passages
the sea still knows the secret of
        and could tell me about
            were I to make you
queen of this northern waste I own:
        as if some part of paradise
unlooked for and unrecognized had been assigned
            worthy of us and of our name

From the measureless sea
up to the rocky beach
with a skirt of ships
        dead of outrageous storm
now dormitories for birds,
        above the beach, green miles,
loud fringe of ceaseless kittiwakes
in spin and squabble on the cliffs,
        snipe overhead
like the great wire I walk on,
sparrows at hide and seek under my feet.
        Survey the meadows
drowning in white orchid
so tall and numerous across the grass
it is as if your thighs
stood multiplied among the blades,
as if you rose
        crowned with weaving birds
to grant a sudden summer to the north.
        In service of your columns
I name this: middle temple of the earth

Sick on this hellbunk all day long
I watch the shadows icebergs make
on walls and ceilings, but do not see the ice.
I give thanks for the whale
that leapt at me enormously just yesterday
and for seeing earth in her waters' arms.
In the ship's bowels I look up at the sky
blindly and know she walks over me
with feet of air and heart of fire
(whom I have pressed into the earth so often)
just as the birds fly over me in dreams
taking their nesting matter from the sunshine

```
                    ...asleep
                              and
        we would come to ourselves in the grass
                        shouting fire
            (as if from a great disaster):
        the purple wave
        of weed would tumble over
        us waking together to the sea –
                              from which
        in a froth like the cloud cap at the pole
                    a whale breaching
        would cross and cross again under the bow
        and his mate, when he had sounded, crossing,
        then sounding, and he crossing,
                        each one each other's shadow –
        that fathomless, out of the blazing grass...
```

Doors of the sea
      closing behind my incapacity,
           the ship
moving into the ocean
         suspended from three stars
with the sun behind her
          dying in Prince William Sound.
Losing her name,
her passengers and destination,
        surge in the night, going,
and about to be lost.
         Interstellar winds
dance with her in far space
our blindness has no conception of:
it has to do with her own lack of title
and purpose at the heart of purpose.
        Morning finds her,
tying her down to schedules
        she'd rather disregard.
           I'm for the night
with all its black disdain of human failure,
  dim details of a coast outside the Sound
where land continues like a broken spine
  willing a body forward though its spirit
has lost all inkling of the sea's direction

To have missed a vocation:
      monk of the sea
waking the islands at daybreak
and putting them to sleep
      as the sun
begins his nightly visit with the dead,
            and further out,
opening and closing the ocean's gates
until the ultimate rim is reached,
            gathering there
all the untethered islands in one flock
      on the black pasture
(where the ice begins)
with their hymns to the sun returning
      and all the marvelous morning
            in my own ears
and in none else…

Dawn.
Birds shearing sea sheep
             close and the
mountain breathing in far mist.
Two hours sail into ash.
The island so untouched
fire grows there on ash
             with its own leaves.
Lazily, immensely high, the mountain
                          sighs and
smokes into unheard of weather.
On the ground, in mid-valley:
                          inua

the mountain's spirit. Fierce
eaglet, terror in the freeze
             over the ashen feathers
a light wind ruffles.
             Only the eye
shutters the inner fire

          Out from this cliff
the sea's daughters lie on their backs
with seals and lions tangled in their hair
each holding an island between her teeth
           foam on her lips:
while the animals, (hell's tier), hell-growl
and the lower earth of Chowiet sweats and shits
          among grass perfumes.
Birds dive
   fighting the upthrust wind,
battling down to their nests
   through funneled tempests,
         the human leg sinks to the hip
and lamely men lurch down into their death
          taking life's pictures.
She forgets, she says,
   everything she has ever known. Only
         the loudest voice counts here
and she has heard it among the other voices
         pulling her down by the roots.
          Sunflare. Beast's breath

Light aura
    around the island
grass on fire
    on the high crests,
crossed knives the walrus
    swaying from side to side
lumbers into the sea,
    more birds than we have ever seen
in our whole lives
    filling the aura with their shadows –
one final day
    life will evidently come to be
this blinding island
              this astonished love

Simeon Ootillian of Sevuokuk
walks out of the morning mist
saying hello how are you after a year
we have not been in or near Sevuokuk
as if he had always expected us
on exactly this day, this ship, this wavelength
of the brotherly mind between us.

        I dream the mountain
should darken the mist with its own looming
and give forth a thousand eiders
for the delectation of my spirit,
the gravel should open of itself under my boots
exposing dark ivory whales.

        Last night in darkness
King Island village thrust out of the vision
we had of a living town, under our searchlight,
handfuls of pointing fingers
mourning for the dead people
frozen in their own breath.

        Simeon Ootillian of Sevuokuk
walks into our poem with Harriet and Job
        newly met today
and all the others we've not yet spoken with.
        The poems are mainly for you

We have left the kingdom of ivory:
                            plow south
through the sea's fields towards St. Paul
                and St. Matthew gives us
a last touch of the white in its own bird
     more snow than the snowbird himself,
all white completely,
                    except the wingtips dipped
in driftwood charcoal.
                        Ink from the sea's own wells
as black as the "lovable Agafon Lestenkov"
whom his father saw clawed down into the dark
                off the bright ice
a century ago it seems to him, at his pulpit,
                   counts the faceless sailors
crawling through his church, watches
     out of a window, the bellowing hills
where the seals also go down into the dark
                    clubbed to a cloud of blood
out of a louring sky

The sailors in love
with animals and birds
      walk into the magic
night of Bogoslov
      with its rock pincers
soaring into the air,
      a sky so pure
   it has never looked down on
any other man than the maker of the island
      Bogoslov –
and in their rapture with the untouched
the sailors wander among the birds
who have never known fear before
      except from other birds.
   In a very few moments
chick after chick of one kind of bird
is eaten by the adults of another kind:
    egg after egg,
          future after future gobbled
among the clenched sunflowers of Bogoslov

On the high grass
above gentle hills
   and the huge bay studded with islands
of a tropical green
               newly enamelled,
   the children of Atka smile
showing all their teeth
   at a moment's relief
from inbreeding.
              I cry metal tears
for all the places
   I shall never see in this life,
clasp you in passionate embrace
while ravens bell overhead,
              roll back and forth
spinning you round and round
while all the earth spins also
and the green ripples like a skin
               over the iron hills

That the earth
         might have claimed a life,
unfinished, green,
                  with no foresight
regarding the end in this huge field
      we finally accredit here –
where we advanced
                         out of the sea
into another sea of lupins
with flecks of iris on a spume
                  of yellow paintbrush,
looking for snowy owl:
                     only to find
   riddled with bullets,
   another kind of bird,
   steel from steel sky,
            who had not forgiven
his unwitnessed fall,
            the interrupted life,
and kept the owls from us

The ship drifts away
from all the continents we know
        into a mapless sea
of uncertain colors –
        but your body remains
anchored among the islands
at the end of this particular earth
        or sits above the weather
like a hawk awake
to any slip or slither in the grass
        my heart might try,
a vole surprised at play,
        when in my ignorance
of where I am, or am likely to be,
(quit of all harbors finally)
I see or sense your smile
        in the round darkness of the void

Alaska, in the Bering Sea, 1977

... after whole days at sea ...

for David Wevill

The ship was
never still
never silent
and never private.
Here in Hokkaido
green waves of silence
climb every hill
and there are white birds
            taking wing
between the crispest sheets.
They glide us into havens
where I can touch you sleeping
and leave my hand on your body

Doves fall
out of the green so
green themselves and
     yellow underneath –
white hortensia,
     shadows in interplays,
bamboo and fir,
       myriad leaf wings.

    Mud underfoot,
cicada mandolin
      about to compose
but looking for a platform
  safe among branches.
We put her up there on a leaf
for safety's sake, for music

Light wakes,
an insistence remembered:
         old sea
in the back dunes of childhood.
         Mountains wait,
capes, just passing flower.
     Can you find, I ask you,
a central corner for these papers
I shall need later from the suitcase
         but not now?
   That is all, you say,
you have ever wanted, isn't it,
         a central corner
in which to store your life?

Play of cloud over Shari
   someone on human feet
must have sung long ago
his voice
   on a human scale exalting the mountain
although objectively
               it isn't very high.
   Meanwhile we two
bullet our way on wheels along
"the only 27 km. of straight road on the island"
towards the "natural flower gardens"
in which the flowers already died
         back in some nameless May
when the poet on foot had prophesied
         an end to the human scale

Ugly streets transformed:
　　　paradise birds dancing,
feathered hats,
　　　tropical fruit dancing,
　cool green drinks
dancing also, wearing shades.
　Thunderbird music,
swordfish drum,
　　　　　beat of delicate hands
　with steel sinews.
　　　　　The wrong clothes
root us to pavements
　　　　　smelling of drains –
　our spirits dance though
in the long oval of the drum's compass
where all the souls invite us,
　even the human bodhisattva,
face uglier than an ugly mask
　he lifts above it to receive his prize

Black Mountain
                Kurodake
climb into clouds
billowing ghosts
sensual to the curve of hills,
        quick in their uplift,
passionate on the wind.
             I am old,
getting too old for mountains,
heart pounds, too many stops –
          while you
  stream up the curves
     a red fox
through monkshood, foxgloves,
           and high up
(remembering another Black Mountain)
      where the flowers shrink
           to small blue stars
I suddenly remember the meaning of
      the traveling life,
my face to the lichens
            in the singing wind

The oldest guide in these parts
        speaks of the stately dance
of guillemots on Teuri.
                Ocean blue women
with long black hair,
        sky beads and gold,
dance as birds in Asahigawa
reminding us of captive cranes
wings far too summer-wet to rise.
                The oldest
   takes your hands,
speaks to you in a dying language
                of air and ice,
   birds and clouds,
sunlight streaming at the sacred window,
the art of growing old gracefully
                still singing…

Rain swallow,
    ama tsubame,
busy time's scythe
    but far faster
slices the air
    above Teuri:
        black knife
through a grey rainbow
made of delicate cloud.
At the busy hour of birds
    all of a sudden
life is tolerable again,
the birds hone to sharpness
    our remembering
that we have never traveled before,
    will not travel again,
are not traveling now.

Hokkaido, Japan, 1977.

Birdscapes with Seaside

In memory of Ivan Morris

"...& *the philosophical light around my window is now my joy; may I be able to keep on as I have thus far!*
—Hölderlin 12.2.1802

It must be to tears
   to the world, dissolving,
it must be to terror,
   inhibitions of thought,
it must be to paralysis
         to the blood quenched
hands fallen asleep
               that it's due –
I had forgotten them:
   and here like clocks come home
               the amenable birds

: :

as long as heart beats
blood diffuses through life
      pacing cold village
there by the creek
            half ice, half water
         brushy stands of seeds
and an attack
         of cardinals, six or as many,
(in the seeming flock):
         rush up the ventricles,
               seizure of sun
                     smiling invisibly

: :

seed
   in itself
       though one year old
still not dead
   breeding very small worms
for the crested tits:
   cat-cradle in air
as they criss cross above
       the seed dispenser
& I wd. have sworn the seed was dead
if there hadn't been, in my mouth,
   a smile sick of repression
yessing the birds today
    back to this hope, this charity

: :

at the very stale
term of all mind,
   old cat dragging its tail along
       like I drag my feet
against the work:
         the craft of thought
   over the abyss
        below this work –
all my years surfacing, all these
           existences
over-familiar with me,
people I've known
never go back to
food like the memory these birds
have no idea they issued from –
   angels / at x per feeder

: :

all back
despite late start so
      bad for business:
the tit forementioned,
purple finch,
gold, chickadee,
      at ground the
whitethroat, junco,
cardinal & jay, and,
      at his drilling,
the woodpecker.
           Nuthatch…
      Where is nuthatch?
      Hatching thought.
  Missing.
Nuthatch nuthatch yourself.
  Forward from origin boy!
Nuthatch. Nuthatch damn it!
      ah, leave be

: :

bird in air
      (the artist arted)
passage to the food
      under the bird,
the air opens
cupped hands hold grace
          unconcealing:
we shld. have been philosophers
I sd. the work begged doing long
ago – the work is light again –
          flight
  to the seed taken back
hammered on branch

                    sweet core
             hungered for so,
long his & ours
                smells in the eaves

: :

sublime pointlessness
of being peep
in flock of peeps
spending a year or two as bird
running to and from tidal waves
picking for cockles
spending the energy as fast as gained
all this under the immense –
so that we name it on our rest
from feeders – cloud of sea, beach, sky,
       sublimest metaphor unless
(my day in the office & yours)
really in the clearing
all is open on all else

: :

blessed power
that has handed down
or caused to happen
  on this dark lake
held in winter's paws
       the class mallard,
the class baldpate,
     or the ruddy duck,
the class black duck

    und so weiter
(all of which duly recorded)
as well as the classes
    never binoculared:
 hooded merganser
comma of water speech,
 canvasback
russet exclamation,
 whistling swan
white question mark
 eyes have not opened on before
anywhere on the stage –
& that thou hast confirmed what is
congruent with its expectations
even if that be science only
    & not yet wisdom

: :

the great birds of the sea
do not to the great ocean down
   & dive he would say
mostly for food
   but for eye's joy
hermit's happiness
    on this lone shore
saint to himself alone –
    but, inasmuch as
they fly in company of kin
 & never solitary
so that their time is a history
   (as we understand it)
thus, it is for the hungry in ourselves,
the humanity which is our nature,
   that, like us, toiling,

they down to smelt & worm,
their lovely passage a banality
              to fill the belly
they and we must march on
                  if we are to grow
legs, wings of willing

: :

the birds
   home from the sea as we are
each in their turn
        draw every branch
in its turn
        to the feeder –
                garden is
drawn
   together, gathered in: *un-*
                 less
the whole garden
        has been gathered first
back from the ocean
        (be it known to you)
& no bird flies from branch,
   no branch springs bird
              to center:
   no rain is water
        that is not wine,
   no seed flour
        that is not bread,
nectar's no drift

: :

the philosopher's
        surface is kind
& easy & it goes
        through all the birds
like a flu –
        how come each bird sounds
unlike itself this morning,
        pecks at the feeders
in unaccustomed ways?
   perhaps they sing
or chirrup in the memory
of the birds of the great sea
        so far behind us now
at anchorage,
        glimpsed for a moment only,
their noise
mere dream as that sea's self
speaks & outreaches
            sail setting sail

: :

at the twelfth hour
   wind round the house
a mindless ocean,
police cars
   radios blaring
(jays & crows)

   jumpy for action but
busting what? preventing what
robbery of imbecile robberibles?

in the huge dark
   we lie, wet worms of light,
for spirit birds to feed on

meantime the smallfry:
   what do they say to all this dying
waiting for breakfast

   as the moon turns and sparks
unforgettable stars
         in the frostrimmed bushes

: :

In the spring rain death's dust rubs off
the bird who has been hidden all winter
like a fire which conspires under embers
needing only a master's touch to flare:
so the gold, understood there all along,
invests the bird at present hardly conscious
of this encroaching beauty. He fans air
under his weight and, more like a sorcerer's
apprentice now, pleasures himself, a boy,
eating the last of winter's grain.
Then notes one morning in his new discretion
he is of the same substance as the sun.

Cape May, New Jersey, 1970s

Publisher's Note

I seem to have a history with some of the contents of this book. 'The Landsongs' was first published in 1980 in *Imprint* magazine, which I co-edited. It then reappeared as a separate small chapbook under the Blue Guitar Books imprint – renamed Shearsman Books shortly afterwards – titled *The Landsongs*, and issued also as part of issue nº 4 of the first series of *Shearsman* magazine in 1981, alongside three other chapbooks.

'Palenque', 'Jonah's Saddle', 'Birdscapes with Seaside' and parts of 'North Rim' appeared in the Shearsman Books / Oasis Books joint publication, *Palenque: Selected Poems 1972–1984* in 1985 (now out of print), which was a selection from the author's first American years for British readers. I've been convinced for quite some time that some of 'North Rim' had previously appeared in *Ninth Decade*, a magazine which I also co-edited back in the '80s and early '90s, but consultation of the back issues proves that my memory has played me false.

In any event, *At the Western Gates* has long been a favourite book of mine and in the 1980s, before the advent of online retailers, it was hard for British readers to find it, or even know that it existed – which is a pity, as it was handsomely produced in an edition of 750 copies by John Brandi's splendidly-named Tooth of Time Books at Santa Fe, New Mexico. This new edition is necessarily less immediately attractive but I am delighted to be able to make it available to a new generation of readers. This edition is expanded by the addition of 'Birdscapes with Seaside', originally published as an issue of *Sparrow* magazine by Black Sparrow Press in 1976.

The Shearsman Library seeks to republish out-of-print books and chapbooks that I think should be made available again. The initial phase contains a dozen books, covering titles by British, American and Australian authors, and its ambition is tempered only by the occasional inability to obtain the necessary rights, or by the fact that another press got there first.

Tony Frazer,
January 2018

www.ingramcontent.com/pod-product-compliance
Lightning Source LLC
Chambersburg PA
CBHW030908170426
43193CB00009BA/773